22 $\frac{60}{}$

My First Pet Library from the **American Humane Association**

My First Horse

American Humane ®

Protecting
Children & Animals
Since 1877

Enslow Elementary
an imprint of

E **Enslow Publishers, Inc.**
40 Industrial Road
Box 398
Berkeley Heights, NJ 07922
USA

http://www.enslow.com

Linda Bozzo

American Humane.

Protecting
Children & Animals
Since 1877

Founded in 1877, the American Humane Association is the oldest national organization dedicated to protecting both children and animals. Through a network of child and animal protection agencies and individuals, the American Humane Association develops policies, legislation, curricula, and training programs to protect children and animals from abuse, neglect, and exploitation. To learn how you can support the vision of a nation where no child or animal will ever be a victim of willful abuse or neglect, visit www.americanhumane.org, phone (303) 792-9900, or write to the American Humane Association at 63 Inverness Drive East, Englewood, Colorado, 80112-5117.

● ●

This book is dedicated to my dad, who learned to never raise his arm too close to a horse, and to my daughter, Macey, for her love and appreciation of horses.

Special thanks to John Degutis for sharing his photographs, Karen Hansen and North Stream Farm, and Spring Valley Equestrian Center and their staff for making their facilities and beautiful horses available to us.

● ●

Copyright © 2008 by Enslow Publishers, Inc.

All rights reserved.

No part of this book may be reproduced by any means without the written permission of the publisher.

Library of Congress Cataloging-in-Publication Data

Bozzo, Linda.
　My first horse / Linda Bozzo.
　　p. cm. — (My first pet library from the American Humane Association)
　Includes bibliographical references and index.
　ISBN-13: 978-0-7660-2753-4
　ISBN-10: 0-7660-2753-8
　1. Horses—Juvenile literature. I. Title.
　　II. Series: Bozzo, Linda. My first pet library from the American Humane Association.
　SF302.B69 2007
　636.1—dc22

　　　　　　　　　　　2006014969

Printed in the United States of America

10 9 8 7 6 5 4 3 2 1

To Our Readers: We have done our best to make sure all Internet Addresses in this book were active and appropriate when we went to press. However, the author and the publisher have no control over and assume no liability for the material available on those Internet sites or on other Web sites they may link to. Any comments or suggestions can be sent by e-mail to comments@enslow.com or to the address on the back cover.

Every effort has been made to locate all copyright holders of material used in this book. If any errors or omissions have occurred, corrections will be made in future editions of this book.

Illustration Credits: ArtToday, Inc., p. 22 (top); Associated Press, pp. 8, 9, 25; Linda Bozzo, pp. 3, 6, 11 (top); © Bob Daemmrich / The Image Works, p. 22 (bottom); John Degutis, pp. 5, 7 (top), 10, 11 (bottom), 12, 13, 14, 15, 16, 18 (left and right), 21 (all), 26; © 2006 Jupiterimages Corporation, p. 17; © ImageState / Alamy, p. 19; Painet, Inc., p. 24; Shutterstock, pp. 1, 4, 7 (middle and bottom), 23, 27, 28, 30.

Cover Credits: Shutterstock

Contents

Horses are Beautiful Animals

Horses are beautiful animals. They need a lot of space and care. Horses can also cost a lot of money to keep. So, hold your horses! You will want to learn everything you can.

Horses are big animals.

This book can help answer questions you may have about finding and caring for your new pet horse.

4

What Kind of Horse Should I Get?

There are many different kinds of horses to choose from. Some horses are good for horse shows. Some are great for trail rides. Maybe you want a horse that will just live in your **pasture**.

You can ride your horse along a trail.

Horses come in
many different
colors.

Arabian horse

Which horse
do you like?

Where Can I Get a Horse?

A great place to get a horse is from a **horse rescue group**. Another good place is a **humane society** that has big animals. A friend that knows about horses might help you pick a horse.

Learn all you can about horses. You could even visit a stable and learn how to take care of a horse.

When picking a horse, it is good to have a **vet** look at the horse. You will want to know how old it is and if it is healthy.

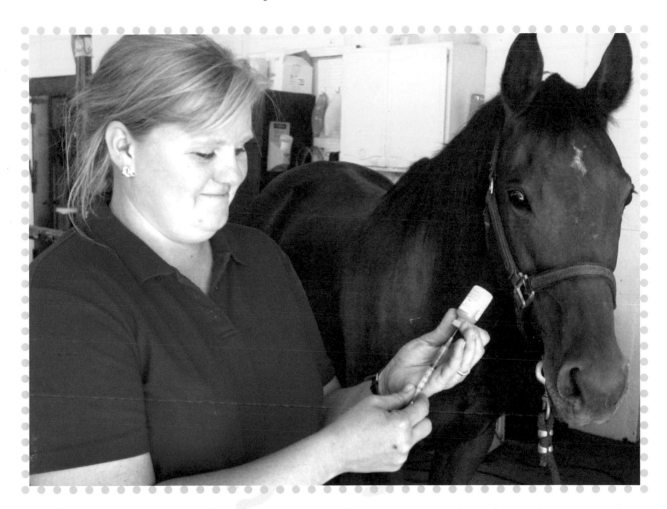

The vet may help you take care of your horse. This vet is going to give the horse a shot.

What Will My New Horse Need?

You will need special brushes and combs to groom your horse. Sponges and cloths are also used to keep your horse clean. A hoof pick is needed for cleaning your horse's feet.

Horse brushes and combs

You need a
lead rope for
your horse.

You need a bridle and
saddle to ride your horse.

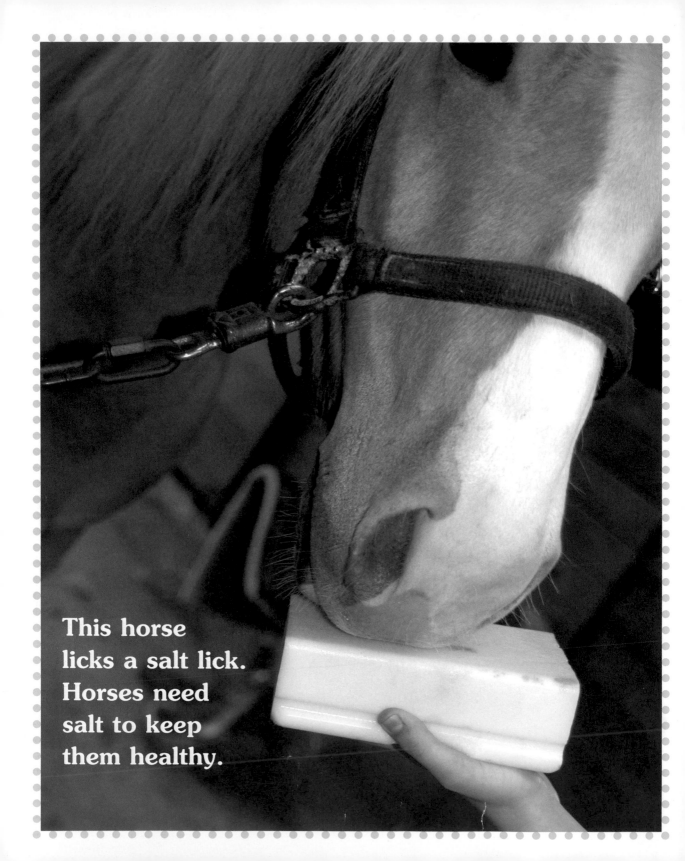

This horse licks a salt lick. Horses need salt to keep them healthy.

You will need feed and water buckets. Storage barrels or bins will help protect the food. A blanket can be used in the winter to keep a horse warm. If you plan to ride your horse you will need things like a **saddle** and **bridle**. A **lead rope** is also important to have.

When it is cold, give your horse a blanket.

What Should I Feed My Horse?

Horses need a very special diet. There are two types of feed. There is **roughage**, which is hay or grass, and there is grain. Ask your vet how much of each type of feed to give your horse. Horses need a

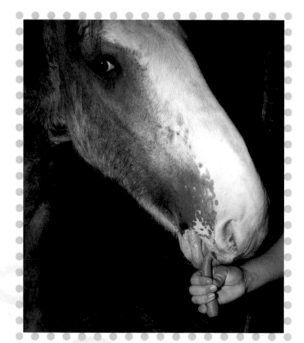

salt or **mineral lick**. Horses also enjoy treats like apples and carrots. Always have clean water where your horse can get to it.

Carrots are healthy treats for a horse.

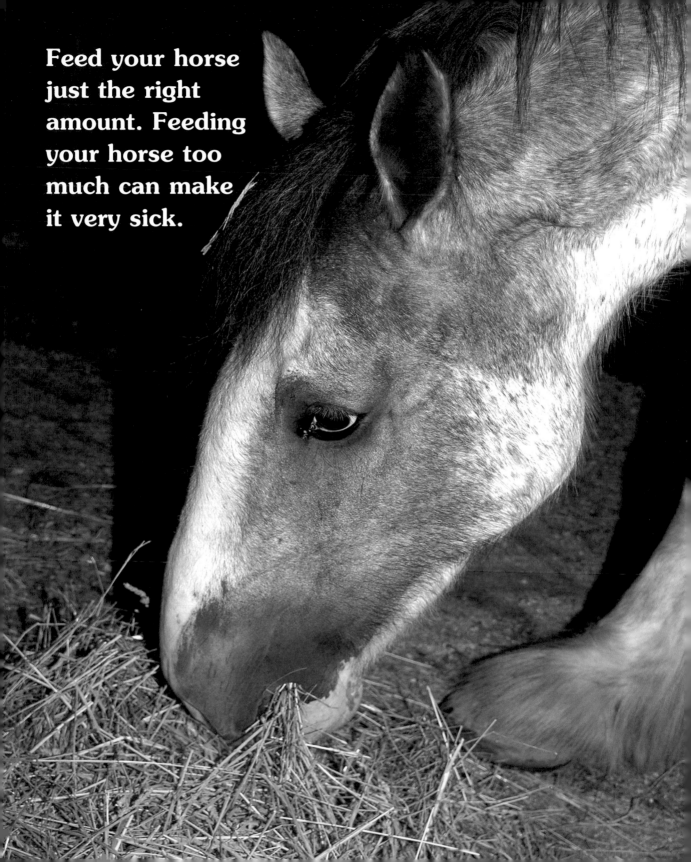

Feed your horse just the right amount. Feeding your horse too much can make it very sick.

This horse eats
a small amount
of food.

Feed your horse at least two times a day. Three times a day is even better. Horses like to eat often in small amounts. Feeding your horse too much can make it sick. Do not work your horse hard right before or after it eats.

Horses like to eat grass.

Where Will My Horse Live?

Horses need to be kept with other horses or they get lonely. They need a shelter like a **stable** or barn. Your horse will need a grassy field to run and graze in. You can board your horse at a stable. This means you will have to pay someone to house your horse.

You can pay someone to keep your horse in their stable.

Your horse can live in a stable.
You can feed and take care of
your horse there.

How Can I Keep My New Horse Healthy and Clean?

Horses must be kept clean by grooming them every day. Special brushes and combs are used to clean your horse's coat. A cloth or sponge is used to groom the head. Use a hoof pick to remove rocks and dirt from the hooves. Horses need horseshoes to protect their hooves. A **farrier** can shoe your horse and trim its hooves.

Sometimes you may need to bathe your horse.

Comb your horse's mane every day.

Use a special brush to clean your horse's body.

21

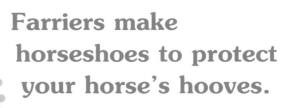

Farriers make horseshoes to protect your horse's hooves.

A horse's stall should be cleaned every day. Horses can get sick if their stalls are not kept clean and dry.

Lead or ride your horse every day.

Letting your horse run around in a field for an hour every day will keep it healthy.

The more your horse runs around, the better. Your horse can run around the field. You should ride or lead your horse every day for at least one hour.

Horses have many ways of showing you they are sick. Your horse may stop eating. Your horse may limp. A sick horse may paw the ground or try to roll. Call your vet right away if you think your horse is sick or hurt.

A vet will help your horse get better if it gets sick or hurt.

Horses need medicine when they get sick, too.
Only a vet should give a horse medicine.

A Great Friend

People of all ages love horses. They are fun to ride. Riding a horse is a great way to stay healthy. Treat your horse well and this beautiful animal will be a great friend.

Horses make great pets and great friends.

Words to Know

bridle—A piece of equipment that fits over the horse's head, used to control the horse.

farrier—A person who fits horseshoes to the horse's feet.

horse rescue group—A group that saves horses and finds them homes.

humane society—An organization that promotes the protection of animals.

lead rope—A rope that is used to lead and tie a horse.

mineral lick—A stone-like block that supplies horses with needed minerals by the horse licking it.

pasture—Land used for grazing.

roughage—Plant material that horses eat, like grass and hay.

saddle—A seat for the rider placed on the back of a horse.

stable—A building where horses are kept.

vet—Vet is short for veterinarian, a doctor who takes care of animals.

Read About

BOOKS

Draper, Judith. *My First Horse and Pony Book*. Boston, Mass.: Kingfisher Publications, 2005.

Gibbons, Gail. *Horses!* New York: Holiday House, 2003.

Holub, Joan. *Why Do Horses Neigh?* New York: Dial Books for Young Readers, 2003.

INTERNET ADDRESSES

The American Humane Association
  <http://www.americanhumane.org>

The American Society for the Prevention of Cruelty to Animals
  <http://www.animaland.org>

Index